Longevity

Lifestyle

Matters

Just the Facts!

Arlene R. Taylor, PhD
with Steve Horton, MPH

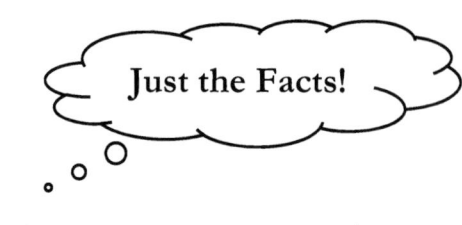

Just the Facts!

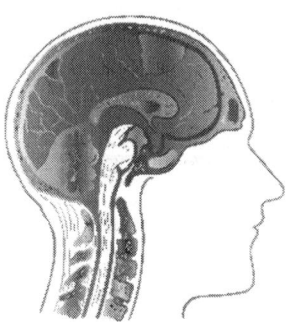

Just the Facts!

Arlene R. Taylor, PhD
with **Steve Horton, MPH**
Success Resources International, Napa, CA

Longevity Lifestyle Matters—Just the Facts

Includes the fourteen strategies presented in the *Longevity Lifestyle Matters* program, outlined in the book *Longevity Lifestyle Matters,* and highlighted at www.longevitylifestylematters.com. Refer to these for additional information or for a refresher.

ISBN # 978-1-887307-07-9

Cover picture by Lawrence Smith, www.bylastingimpressions.com

Cover design by David O. Eastman
Printed in the United States of America

Dedication

This book is dedicated to all those who asked for ***Just the Facts*** as a quick reminder of key points to help them keep their *Longevity Lifestyle* on track—because it *Matters*! The goal, of course, is to stay healthier and younger for longer. Hopefully your brain will capture a new "Ah-ha" perspective regarding the brain, health, wellness, and longevity.

Acknowledgement

No one is an island. None writes a book alone. Many people deserve a sincere "thanks" for their ideas, encouragement, and enthusiasm, all of which added a huge dose of *fun* to the process!

Here are just a few:

- Steve Horton for brainstorming ideas
- Michelle Nash for copy editing
- Brenda Balding for wording suggestions
- Daniel Mendez for Internet assistance
- Michael Hudson for executive production of the audiobook and music composition

Publisher's Reminder

Just the Facts is provided for general educational and informational purposes only and does not present an in-depth treatment of specific research findings or topics. The information is not intended to take the place of professional counseling, medical or psychological care, recovery therapy, or personalized recommendations from healthcare professionals. Since every brain is different, there are no guarantees of individual results.

Be sure to consult your physician or other healthcare professionals before you make lifestyle changes or implement new exercise strategies. The publisher, authors, contributors, reviewers, editors, certified facilitators, or volunteers expressly disclaim all responsibility and any liability whatsoever (direct or indirect) for outcomes or adverse effects (actual or perceived), from use, misuse, or inappropriate application of concepts presented herein.

If you find errors or typos, please know that they do serve a purpose. Making mistakes is part and parcel of being human—and some brains really enjoy looking for mistakes.

Table of Contents

"If you keep on doing what you are doing, you will keep on getting what you are getting...

—George E. Guthrie, MD, MPH

Introduction

What is the reason for this little book?

Because we **listened**!

Individuals who have read (or listened to) the *Longevity Lifestyle Matters* (*LLM*) books or attended the 12-week, brain-based *LLM* program asked for a short summary of Facts that highlighted a few key points on each of the 14 components or strategies. Those who requested *Just the Facts* offered two main reasons:

First: To carry around with them as both a *reminder* and a *review* of key components in the longevity lifestyle they personally created and are choosing to follow for the rest of their lives. If this is new for you, think of it as a *preview* of the LLM program and the longer books that offer more in depth stories for each of the components.

Second: To share with others in the hope that they will *also* be motivated to take better care of the brain and body leased to them for use on this planet. As one person put it: a desire for loved ones to "still be around so we can grow older together." Not every person who becomes acquainted with LLM will choose to embrace a healthier lifestyle. However, brains exposed to a new idea never return to their original dimensions. As such, if someone makes even the *smallest* of changes, every positive improvement matters in what is known as *life*.

In the beginning, the impetus for the *LLM* books and the *LLM* program was based on the staggering prediction that this generation may be the first to live shorter lives than their parents. Evidence is seen daily in epidemics and pandemics currently raging on this planet, including . . .

- Heart Disease and Stroke
- More than 200 types of Cancer
- Diabetes and Lung Diseases
- Anxiety Disorders including Depression
- Overweight and Obesity
- Alzheimer's and other dementias
- Infectious and Communicable Diseases

But it quickly became more than that. Research is revealing that how well and how long you live is due less to the impact of Genetics (an estimated 30 percent) and far more to Epigenetics (an estimated 70  percent)—your personal *lifestyle* choices. In adulthood, all of which begin in your brain!

No parent—*no* friend, *no* acquaintance—wants to experience debilitating chronic diseases personally or in those they love. Unfortunately, the way many people are living—perhaps even you?—has proven unsuccessful in helping them stay "healthier and younger for longer." This often includes choices based on what they experienced in childhood or—if they didn't like the way they were raised—180 degrees different. However, 180 degrees from dysfunctional is still dysfunctional. For many, there was no easily accessible body of knowledge to help them create and follow a personalized longevity lifestyle.

For some, pulling one's head out of the sand may be the *first* helpful solution. The brain harbors many perceptions regarding health, lifestyle, lifespan, and wellness—often absorbed prior to age five. Such views may embody long-standing, deeply entrenched habits and generational beliefs about well-being. While altering such may be a challenge,  it is *a doable* task. Fortunately, research is demonstrating simple strategies to reduce one's risk for illness, disease, and a shortened lifespan.

LLM embraces the exponential power of science to work with both the brain and body. It is designed to help you pursue gradual and permanent lifestyle changes to *prevent* what is preventable, *reduce the risk* for what is not preventable, and *manage more effectively* what was not—or could not be—prevented.

Fourteen components have been identified to help you stay "healthier and younger" for longer. Sometimes these strategies can even reverse deficits that occurred due to lack of knowledge and/or poor personal choices and decisions. Each strategy links back to the brain in some way: after all, *everything* begins in the brain. Every chapter highlights bits of researched information, broken down into bite-sized "facts" that you can turn into knowledge and practically apply preventatively on a daily basis.

A selected bibliography is included in the larger *Longevity Lifestyle Matters* book for those who want to delve more deeply into the facts. There, the facts are presented in story form about real people who learned how to stay healthier and younger for longer, sometimes even restoring specific deficits. (An audiobook is also available in CD and MP3 formats.)

A large sign posted on the wall of a hospital's Emergency Department reads: *Those who are too busy to take care of their health are like mechanics who are too busy to take care of their "tools.*

What are *your* "tools"? Your brain and body, of course. You need a healthy body to carry around your brain, along with a well-functioning brain to make doing that worthwhile. You and your brain *can* put together the puzzle pieces. Current collective wisdom highlights the importance of taking personal responsibility for yourself and for using your *tools* (i.e., proactive, thoughtful, and preventive maintenance) on a daily and ongoing basis.

Your brain and immune system work hand-in-glove to keep you well and, if you get sick, to help you heal. Together, they constitute the most amazing healing system on Planet Earth—maybe in the known Universe. They are, however, impacted by nature and nurture: genetics and epigenetics. Especially by epigenetics because that includes all lifestyle factors.

The goal is to raise the bar on your state of well-being and keep it as high as possible for as long as you live. Embracing longevity-lifestyle strategies as part of your daily, ongoing choices can make a positive difference in your life—*and* in the lives of those you love and care about . . . *and* in the lives of those who love and care about you!

 Starting *now* is not a minute too soon. Time to get cracking—in a manner of speaking.

Lifestyle *matters!*

Want to be healthy? Here's where to begin.
In your brain, of course—where you lose or win.
Prevention strategies you devise,
Can help you live longer and healthfully wise.

"Mornin', Ms Mahetabel," said Robinson Crusoe. "Another fine day, don't you know."

"Cain't you see I'm busy?" clucked Ms Mahetabel. "I've a mind to cross this road."

"What's wrong with some chick-chat while you're waiting?" asked Crusoe. "For example, which do you think came first, the chicken or the egg?"

"Don't know—what's more, don't care," clucked Ms Mahetabel. "These here feathers are lookin' for treasure on yon side of the road."

"Well, think about this," Crusoe went on, undeterred. "Cars create traffic—then traffic impacts cars, helping or impeding their progress and influencing their travel. Think about it."

"Told you. I'm in a flurry of a hurry!" clucked Ms Mahetabel, ruffling her feathers. "No time to think."

"Well, since there's no break in traffic, you may as well improve your tiny brain," said Crusoe. "Try this one. Brain creates mind—then mind impacts brain, facilitating or impeding its functions and influencing health and longevity."

"What a twit!" clucked Ms Mahetabel "I'm crossing this road NOW! Traffic or no tr … __"

"Ah, me," Robinson Crusoe sighed. "There goes another brainless bird…"

The Fact Is …

Nature plus Nurture = You

Nature involves Genetics

Genetics represents the "stuff" you inherit from your biological parents and is responsible for about 30 percent of who you are. It includes your chromosomes and genes. Chromosomes are single-coiled strands of deoxyribonucleic acid [DNA], nucleic acids [RNA], and proteins, made of amino acids. A 1962 Nobel Prize was awarded for the discovery of the elegant molecular structure of DNA, known as the double helix. Estimates are that 99 percent of your DNA is located in your chromosomes. The remaining one percent is found in the mitochondria, tiny energy factories inside cells that have a clearly defined nucleus. The mitochondria create adenosine triphosphate [ATP], the energy source needed to power almost all cellular activity.

Genes are tiny bits of DNA that contain "blueprints" (architectural plans) for creating three-dimensional building blocks from proteins. About 25,000 genes, contained in your chromosomes, determine your inherited traits such as body build and height, male or female, the color of your hair, eyes, and skin, the potential talents that you can hone, and so on.

1

Estimates are that during the first trimester, more than 95 percent of embryos form correctly, based on the genetic blueprints. Those that do not form correctly may exhibit a birth defect. By the end of the first 12 weeks, the initial construction of body organs is in place. These include the brain, heart, lungs, digestive system, liver, kidneys, the circulatory system (with its arteries, veins, and capillaries), and the immune system along with its immune vessels and lymph nodes. The brain, however, 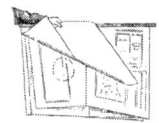 continues to develop throughout pregnancy with neurons being created at the rate of 250,000 per minute. More than half of all fetal metabolic energy is devoted to growing the brain, which will continue to develop/mature for years after the fetus is born.

To recap: nature involves *genetics,* your g*enome*—the genes and chromosomes inherited from biological parents. The genes contain "blueprints" for the building blocks of life. Created from proteins, they include those needed for repair of cellular structures and for the replication of cells. Many factors, however, influence how blueprints are "read" and interpreted and implemented.

Nurture **involves Epigenetics**

In the word *epigenetics,* "epi" means "above." *Above genetics.* It accounts for about 70 percent of your level of wellness and lifespan. Think of epigenetics as everything that is not genetics: the sum total of your internal and external environments, beginning with conception and continuing with a calm or stressful gestation, along with a pleasant or traumatic birth experience, the memory of which likely is lodged in your subconscious memory. Epigenetics has a definite impact on the process of gestation— and may kick in earlier than previously believed.

Vital nutrients are carried from the placenta to the fertilized ovum via the umbilical cord, which also transmits hormones and chemicals carried in the blood that provide information about what is happening to the mother physically and emotionally. In whatever way the mother experiences her internal and external environments—dreadful or delightful—the fetus will share the impact of the mother's experiences. This, in turn, can influence how the building blocks of life are constructed.

Uterine scans have identified four core emotions that can be seen on the face of the fetus reflecting what the mother is experiencing emotionally: joy, anger, fear, or sadness. The fetus is believed able to sense her emotions, along with whether or not it is wanted, and if it is the gender the parent(s) would prefer. If both biological parents are present and are a supportive team, this will impact the mother's emotional wellbeing positively. If the parents are unhappy about the pregnancy or if the father physically or emotionally abandons the biological mother, the fetus will sense the mother's distress. If the maternal and paternal family systems are excited about the pregnancy and are waiting to welcome the newborn with open arms—or not—either way, the fetus will sense that and learns about the potential safety or danger in the external environment from this epigenetic information.

When the mother perceives something as stressful, the stress response is triggered automatically and substances such as adrenalin and cortisol flood her body. Her developing fetus receives that information, too. If the stress response is triggered frequently the fetus can become hyper-sensitive and reactive to any type of event or situation that its brain perceives as stressful. This pattern can continue after birth, resulting in a tendency to *overreact* in stressful situations. (Note: once the stress response is triggered it can take up to 72 hours for the body to return to a state of "homeostasis" or balance.)

And it's *not* just maternal stress that can impact the developing fetus. Studies with mice led by Tracy Bale, PhD, at the University of Maryland, School of Medicine, have shown that negative and/or chronic stressors can alter the father's sperm, which then can alter the brain development of the child.

Metaphorically, imagine 100,000 tiny switches on the surface of cell membranes that relay signals (information) from the environment to components inside the cell. By this means epigenetics can impact how genetic blueprints are "read" and interpreted and how the building blocks of life are assembled.

Epigenetics may also help to explain the "rage" that some abandoned, foster, surrogate, or adopted children exhibit. Their new environments may be very different from the environments it became accustomed to during gestation. Healthy or unhealthy, it was familiar: smells, tastes, sounds, touch, music, and sometimes language, race, culture, or even location on the planet. A disconnection from what was familiar can be stressful, unsettling, and terrifying—if not "mind blowing"—for the child.

But hang on a minute. There is another component to epigenetics: your *perceptions.* Each person develops a mindset that Carol S. Dweck, PhD, describes as usually either "fixed" or "growth." Your *perceptions* come from your mindset and impact how you *perceive* and *interpret* life. Perceptions start forming during gestation and continue throughout life. In adulthood, you can review your perceptions: analyze them, keep some, dump some, tweak some, and create new ones. You can alter your mindset and your perceptions—negatively or positively—which impacts epigenetic signals that are transmitted to components inside your cells, which influence how genetic blueprints are read and interpreted, and how building blocks are fashioned and repaired.

To recap: nurture involves *epigenetics* (your *epigenome*), responsible for about 70 percent of who you are and powerful enough to even alter genetics. Epigenetics is everything that is not genetics. It includes what happens to you, the choices you make, the habits you develop, the behaviors you exhibit, the stressors you are exposed to and how you respond, your job or career, and your relationships, both personal and professional. Epigenetics includes your lifestyle: what you eat and drink, where you go, what you do, whom you hang out with, what you listen to, what you read, what you watch, the sports you play, and the music you like, to name a few.

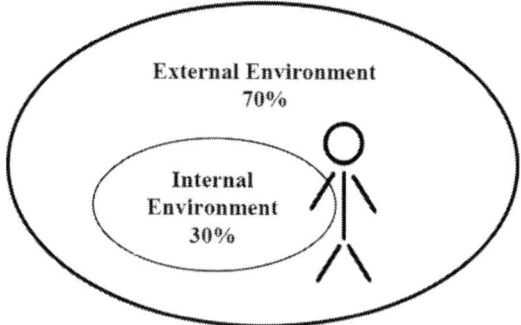

Research about genetics and epigenetics is growing by leaps and bounds and what is being discovered is making space fantasies look rather elementary.

A common perception for generations was that a newborn's brain entered the world as a relatively blank slate. Current wisdom has turned that upside down. It is now believed that a newborn brain is far more developed, aware, and perceptive than anyone ever imagined! This tiny brain can remember voices, songs, and stories it heard during gestation; understand a great deal of spoken language, communicate easily through sign language long before speech is produced; and learn two or three different languages simultaneously.

Who you are as a unique individual involves complex *interactions* among your brain and spinal cord, your genome and epigenome, your microbiome and virome (bacteria and viruses—good and bad—that live inside you), along with the cellular memories of behaviors from three or four generations of biological ancestors. Which means, as William Faulkner put it, the past is never dead. It's not even past! You carry it within you.

This relatively new body of knowledge about biology may help explain how specific diseases and behaviors occur more often in some family systems: cancer or heart disease, diabetes or strokes, lung problems or liver failure, and addictive behaviors. And it is clarifying what you can and cannot change in this complex nature-nurture equation.

You arrived on Planet Earth with a genetic biological inheritance: your *genome*, responsible for about 30 percent of your level of wellness and your potential lifespan. You didn't place an order for your specific genome—but it's *yours!* You experienced both internal and external environments during gestation, childhood, and adulthood: your *epigenome.* In adulthood, you make choices (little and large) every day that create your lifestyle—and it's *yours!*

Lifestyle has a much greater impact on health and longevity than was thought possible. The choices you make impact epigenetics—negatively or positively—which impact your level of health and wellness and your potential longevity.

You can't change the past, but you can create a healthier future! How can you do this?

Learn what you can about your genetic inheritance, as strategies may be available to reduce your risk for some illnesses and diseases. *Identify* your mindset and personal perceptions and course correct as needed. *Develop* a longevity lifestyle and prevent what is preventable. *Handle* more effectively what was not or could not be prevented. *Choose* wisely, making decisions based on informed evaluations. *Use* willpower to help you create and sustain new behaviors successfully.

According to Daniel M. Wegner, PhD, willpower was not designed to help you stop a "bad" behavior, especially one that gives your brain some type of reward. Willpower was designed to help you persevere in developing healthier and more functional behaviors that result in positive outcomes.

Stop talking about the old behavior and talk only about the new behaviors you are embracing—then implement them consistently. Creating "better" behaviors successfully requires: a growth mindset, helpful self-talk, rehearsal of healthier choices, willpower, and vigilance—and it can be done.

Due to an updated understanding of biology, *Just the Facts* is designed to help you manage epigenetics more effectively. Fourteen epigenetic components are highlighted over which you can have partial—if not complete—control. They are:

Mindset	Safety
Self-talk	Sunlight
EQ	Nutrition
Physical Exercise	Laughter
Brain Stimulation	Support System
Optimum Sleep	Stress Management
Essential Hydration	Life Satisfaction

Do you want to stay healthier and younger for longer?

Sign *on,* dig *in*—and get *going*. It *matters!*

So how in the "health" are you?
Could you be better? What's your view?
If the answer is yes, then pitch right in—
Right now is the best time to begin…

"Did you know that 30 percent of endangered species never hatch?" cheeped the 1st egg. "That's 3 of every 10 eggs that will never see the light of dawn, twice the rate of regular species. I fear I'll be in the 30 percent—and that's going to make for a very short cramped life!"

"Of all the ridiculous bird-brained notions I ever heard tell of, yours takes the complete yoke!" cheeped the 2nd egg.

"It's not ridiculous," squawked the 1st egg. "It's just a crap shoot, that's what it is. I'm history. I feel it in my shell and in my yoke."

"You and your shell and your yoke," the 2nd egg cheeped. "If you think you can or you think you can't—either way, you're right."

"I think I *can't*," said the 1st egg. "I'm endangered and my shell is just too hard."

"Me? I have a different opinion," cheeped the 2nd egg. "I plan to be in the 70 percent that *does* hatch, which is seven of every ten eggs."

"What's that infernal noise?" cheeped the 1st egg.

Me, of course," cheeped the 2nd egg, merrily. "I've decided that right now is the best time to get cracking! If it's too loud for you, try sticking your head under your wing. Or, on second thought, we could make it a cracking duet!"

1—Mindset

Fact. Everything begins in your brain! Your thoughts create your mindset—the lens through which you identify, perceive, respond to, and act upon what happens inside and outside of you. A metaphorical map for your brain to follow. Life experiences can influence the type of mindset you develop, but no one can actually create it *for* you—that's up to you. The choices you make automatically (or by conscious consideration) are influenced by your mindset. Dr. Carol Dweck describes two general types: a *fixed* mindset—"I am what I am, and there's little if anything I can do about it—-and a *growth* mindset—"My brain can learn and improve. It's my job to make that happen. I'm on it!"

Fact. Henry Ford nailed it: "Whether you think you can or whether you think you can't, you're right." Only one idea can occupy the brain's working memory at a time. Negative thoughts trigger the recall of negative memories. Positive thoughts flood working memory with positivity, triggering recall of constructive memories. Either *you* choose to control your mindset or outside factors *will*—and your mindset makes all the difference.

Fact. Negativity rarely (if ever) solves anything. Usually it creates even more problems, triggering the stress response. Once a stress response has been activated, it may take 72 hours for the body to return to a state of homeostasis (balance)—*if* effective stress-management strategies are implemented. Here's the bad news: the length of the stress response can be extended by ruminating on undesirable aspects of a situation, especially if you frequently choose to give Broadway-winning performances, repeating your discontent to anyone who will listen. However, if you think of something for which to be grateful, that will be the focus of your brain's working memory. Studies have shown that fear and thankfulness cannot co-exist simultaneously in the brain. In other words, *gratitude* trumps fear.

Fact. Mindset alters your neurochemistry which, in turn, impacts your immune system. Mindset also influences everything from happiness and wellness to success and longevity. Although mindset happens internally, what occurs outside your brain and body tends to mirror what is happening on the inside. In other words, your mindset has a way of aligning in harmony with either the negative *or* the positive. Those who are truly successful are known for being able to move from mistake to mistake (as all humans do) with no loss of enthusiasm. You are the only person who can change your mindset—and sometimes just doing that can make all the difference in the world—even shortening or lengthening your life. In the process, if you choose a growth mindset, your rate of making mistakes may decrease even as your rate of success increases.

Fact. It is estimated that at least half the problems humans experience are of their own making—based on the way they *think*. That's mindset. If you have an enemy outpost of negativity inside your brain, dump it! Unmanaged negative stress is said to be the precursor of *all* life-threatening illnesses. *Can't, don't, won't, couldn't,* and/or *shouldn't* thinking patterns are deadly to success. Negativity adversely impacts *all* your relationships. It also cripples a long, happy, healthy, and productive life. Learn to recognize negative and disempowering thoughts and replace them with positive *can-do* thoughts.

Fact. Your mindset generates your self-talk… which impacts the emotions that arise…which affects your choices… which drives your behaviors… which influences the course of your life in every way imaginable. You are the only person who can flip the switch from a *fixed* to a *growth* mindset, creating either an undesirable or a desirable cascade. Remaining healthier and younger for longer *is* possible, and it all begins in your brain.

Fact. Mindset *matters*!

**Mindset is your own GPS,
A guidance system toward success.
It helps you think and then to choose
The strategies that you will use.**

"My arrows keep hitting the ground!" whined Archer One for the umpteenth time. "Your arrows *don't* hit the ground. What's with that?"

"I suppose it could be most anything," replied Archer Two, pulling an arrow from the quiver and fitting it to the bow. The arrow hit the target right at the edge of the bull's eye.

"It has to be my equipment!" continued Archer One. "Maybe it is the bow...or perhaps the arrows... Doubt it would be the quiver!"

"Near as I can tell there's only one difference between us," replied Archer Two, mildly, "and it has nothing to do with equipment. I always begin by telling myself: 'Archer Two, you aim high. You hit the target.' Maybe if you dumped whining and blaming, changed your self-talk, and aimed higher—your arrows just might take flight and hit the target, too."

"If you aren't just the most unhelpful person in the world!" complained Archer One. "And here you're supposed to be a good friend!"

"I'm *trying* to be just that," said Archer Two. "A good friend. I really do think that if you simply changed . . . . ."

"Oh, save your breath," snapped Archer One. "I'm outta here . . . it's very obvious that archery just ain't my game."

2—Self-talk

 **Fact.** Self-talk is a label for what human beings—including you—tell themselves internally or aloud. Self-talk springs from your mindset, your beliefs, and what people tell you or what you hear them say about you. It has a huge impact on your life by creating your reality, influencing your thoughts and feelings, and triggering your behaviors. Negative self-talk is most *un*helpful and can lead to discouragement, self-pity, a sense of hopelessness or helplessness, failure, and depression. Positive self-talk helps you achieve your goals, including happiness and health, enhanced relationships, and a potential increase in longevity.

Fact. Your brain can only do what it thinks it can do—and your job is to inform what it can do. Your subconscious listens to and believes what you say *to* and *about* yourself. It doesn't use language per se,

> *Affirmation is the mind's programming language.*
> —Jean Marie Stine

but it does tend to see and follow the pictures your self-talk creates. It believes that *if* you said it and *if* you pictured it, you must want it. Therefore, it creates a mental picture in your working memory of what it thinks you want to happen. Avoid using words like *can't* and *don't* and *won't*, as they create negative pictures. Switch to a self-talk style that uses positive, present-tense words to communicate with your brain. Give your brain *positive* instructions to achieve *positive* outcomes. If you dislike what is happening, change your self-talk. Positivity is critically important.

Fact. Positive self-talk--both less stressful and more effective--also reduces anxiety, and requires less electrical activity. Stop telling yourself what you do not want to happen and talk only about what you do want to happen—as if it's already a done deal. Learn positive self-talk patterns that use *short, positive* phrases and sentences in the *present tense.* Speak to your brain as a separate entity—because it pretty much is. Use your first name and the pronoun *you: "Jack (or Jill), you give your brain positive instructions only."*

Fact. Metaphorically, the brain tends to put its shoulder to the wheel based on what is happening in the present moment. When you say, "I am going to," or "Starting tomorrow," or "After the holidays," the brain's neocortex registers the future tense and does little—if anything—to help you. Imagine it is thinking: *That is then but this is now. When 'then' arrives, I'll help you. But based on past experience, you likely will have forgotten all about it. Just think of all the time and energy I will have saved!*

Fact. The body's energy is closely connected with mindset, self-talk, and the internal mental pictures these create. Positive self-talk patterns strengthen the immune system and increase energy levels, while negative thoughts and feelings deplete energy. Anxiety and anger are energy eaters. A negative self-talk style can turn into a vicious cycle that drags you down. Pay attention—since all you are is *energy*! A positive self-talk style brings an extra bonus, since studies show that you tend to communicate with others in the way you talk to yourself. Get your brain in gear and learn to speak to yourself as you would  to your best friend. Matter of fact, *be* your own best friend. After all, the only person who will be with you for your entire life is *you*. So, you may as well become your best friend! As you learn to speak positively to yourself, you'll tend—almost automatically—to use that same style with others.

Fact. The most effective formula for behavior change is positive self-talk followed by consistent and ongoing practical application. Forgive yourself for your mistakes, learn from them, course-correct, and move on. What you tell yourself and how you frame it makes all the difference in the world.

Fact. Self-talk *matters!*

Affirmations can program your brain,
To help you succeed and your goals attain.
Tell your brain what it needs to do:
Plan—by design—so your dreams come true.

"So, tell me how your catnip party went," said Boots. "Did you and Kit have a good time?"

"I had a *great* time," replied Kat. "I've no idea what Kit did. I did not, did NOT, invite her."

"Didn't invite your best friend to your catnip party?" asked Boots. "What's with that?"

"*Was!*" exclaimed Kat. "Nobody walks by and ignores *me* and gets away with it. Nobody!"

"Seems like a colossal overreaction," said Boots.

"That's as may be," said Kat, "but Kit is history!"

"Behaviors don't come out of a vacuum," said Boots. "Call Kit and ask what happened. That would be the emotionally intelligent thing to do."

"Nope, she's out of my life—I'm done," said Kat. "I hope she's moved on. I sure have."

(Fast forward a couple weeks)

"You were right," sighed Kat. "I jumped to conclusions, overreacted, took things personally, and burned my bridges with Kit. I found out she didn't even see me—she'd just heard her Ma has cancer. Most unfortunate!"

Hmm-m, mused Boots, to himself. *Those JOT behaviors are really quite costly...*

3—Emotional Intelligence

 **Fact.** Your Emotional Intelligence Quotient (EQ)—skills to help you manage emotions, feelings, and relationships—is vitally important to success in every area of life, both personal and professional. Most people would like a high success quotient (SQ). Your overall success is a combination of your IQ plus your EQ. However, IQ only contributes 20 percent to your SQ, while EQ contributes 80 percent—making EQ your "ace in the hole" for your SQ. While a potential IQ range is inherited, EQ skills must be *developed.*

Fact. Emotions (triggered by internal *or* external stimuli) connect the subconscious with the conscious mind, offering both *information* and *energy.* In the grip of a strong emotion, the brain (seeking congruity) recalls past events that involved a similar emotion, intensifying the present emotion. High levels of EQ help you identify core emotions quickly and accurately, recognize the information they are providing, and manage them effectively—along with the feelings created by your brain's interpretation of the emotion. If you don't like the way you *feel*, change the way you *think* and what you *tell yourself.* While you are not responsible for every emotion triggered by a stimulus, typically you can choose the feelings to hang onto long term since your brain creates feelings to explain emotions.

Fact. Four core emotions have been observed on fetal faces during uterine scans, based on what is happening with the mother. All core emotions are positive, even though the behaviors exhibited around them may be quite negative. *Joy* tells you that life is going well and that you have the tools to solve problems. PET scans have shown that joy lights up the brain's left hemisphere. The other three core "protective" emotions light up the right hemisphere. *Anger* informs when boundaries have been invaded so you can create—or reset—and maintain bona fide boundaries. *Fear* warns that you may be in some type of danger, unless triggered by imagined fears. *Sadness* alerts you to a loss, so you can identify it, move through the grieving process, recover, and feel better again.

Fact. High levels of EQ skills help you evaluate a situation quickly and accurately and determine what action (if any) is needed. You learn to estimate how much a given event or situation will matter in twelve months. If the probability is high, start problem-solving immediately. If low, open your mind's door and let it go. When asked for your opinion, high EQ skills allow you not only to share as honestly and graciously as possible, but also to remain relatively indifferent as to whether your opinion is even accepted. This helps you avoid badgering others to embrace your perspective. No one brain knows everything, so input from differing brains can increase the likelihood of a more optimum solution.

Fact. Low levels of EQ skills can contribute to all manner of messes (some worse than others) that generally need to be cleaned up. Three common behaviors tend to represent low levels of EQ and contribute heavily to conflict and misunderstanding in personal as well as professional relationships. Taylor has defined them as **JOT** behaviors:

- **J**umping to Conclusions
- **O**verreacting
- **T**aking Things Personally.

How do you minimize JOT behaviors and build higher levels of EQ skills? By implementing replacement **AAA** behaviors:

- **Ask** questions to clarify—instead of jumping to a conclusion that may be way off base.
- **Act** calmly as you assess the situation—to prevent a reactive emotional tsunami.
- **Alter** your perception or reframe the event— to avoid taking things personally.

Fact. Emotional Intelligence *matters!*

> **EQ is your very best friend.**
> **Your success it can extend.**
> **Triple A can prevent JOTs,**
> **In children, adults—even tots.**

"Exercise time," Goatee announced. "Our spring climb to the Arctic Circle starts in a few weeks."

"No rush," said little Nutmeg, stretching. "No point getting my whiskers in a knot just yet."

Cinnamon, Nutmeg's twin, asked, "What's the best exercise for this climb?" Hearing Goatee's reply, Cinnamon immediately began a practice routine of jumping up onto a flat rock and back down again—and again and again.

"How are the legs coming, Nutmeg?" Goatee asked a few days later. "It's quite a climb!"

"Got it handled," said Nutmeg, yawning. "Plenty of time yet to get exhausted."

Cinnamon easily kept up with Goatee as they headed for the Arctic Circle, the rest of the herd strung out behind. "Oh, there you are," said Goatee, when Nutmeg straggled in toward the end of an afternoon respite. "Do try to keep up. It's unsafe to lag. Predators and all."

"Suppose I could have worked out a bit more," panted Nutmeg. "Pace is a bit brisk for me..."

Use it or lose it, Cinnamon thought to himself. *Sure glad I put in the exercise time—even though it was hard work!*

Once at the Arctic Circle, Nutmeg was nowhere to be seen...never did show up. Pity, that...

4—Physical Exercise

 **Fact.** Physical exercise is vitally important for both brain and body. It strengthens the heart, bolsters the immune system, boosts energy, relieves stress, enhances cognition, and improves sleep. The value of exercise has *less* to do with building muscles or burning calories and *more* to do with getting the heart to pump faster and more efficiently, thereby increasing blood flow to nourish and cleanse the brain and body organs.

Fact. The exercise of large muscle groups facilitates the return of blood to the heart through the veins and lymph fluid through the lymph vessels. Blood circulates through the body at least once a minute—and sometimes two or three times a minute depending on your heart rate and your activity. Each day, every cell in the blood travels the equivalent of nearly half-way around Planet Earth at its equator! When operating correctly, the circulatory system is a very effective two-way distribution system. It delivers oxygen, glucose, and other essential micronutrients to each cell. In turn, it picks up carbon dioxide, carrying it (and other waste products) away.

Fact. Studies of senior citizens who walk regularly (as compared to sedentary elderly persons) showed improvement in memory skills, learning ability, concentration, and abstract reasoning. According to

Candace B. Pert, PhD, twenty minutes of mild aerobic exercise at the beginning of the day turns on fat-burning neuropeptides, the effects of which can last for hours. This can be critical in managing diseases such as obesity and diabetes. *Brain Rules* explains that upping your daily exercise to a 20-minute walk could cut stroke risk by 57 percent.

Fact. Minimize *sitting* and maximize physical activity. If you are doing largely sedentary work, do some standing at a raised desk, if possible. Move around for a couple of minutes every half hour, setting a timer if need be. Aim to exercise for 30 minutes each day, possibly in sections of 10 or 15 minutes if that works better for your schedule. Include a combination of stretching, aerobics, endurance, balance, and flexibility exercises.

Fact. Willpower can be defined as the energetic determination to carry out your chosen plans and decisions. It is a brain function designed to help you create a brand new behavior. Willpower is not designed to stop bad habits, especially those that give you a hit in the Brain Reward System. Picture in your mind's eye what you want to do for exercise, then use willpower to help you actually and do it.

Fact. Use it and move it or *lose* it—but choose your physical activities and exercise routines with care. The advice of Hippocrates still stands: *Do no harm.* For example, after decades of being touted as beneficial, jogging (when compared with walking or running) is getting mixed reviews for the average person. Over time, jogging can damage joints, stretch ligaments, and may even compound cellulite. If you enjoy intensity training, alternate several minutes of brisk walking, biking, rowing or swimming with several minutes of more moderate exercise. If you are accustomed to being sedentary, consult your physician or other healthcare professional before beginning an exercise program.

Fact. Physical exercise is an anti-aging strategy. Variety is key to keeping your brain interested and motivated, so select activities and exercises you enjoy. Be creative. You need a healthy body to carry your brain around, and you want a healthy brain while your body is transporting it hither and yon. Even small changes can contribute to enhanced health and longevity. Nearly everyone can find a way to obtain the physical activity and exercise their brains and bodies require. Concentrate on what you *can* do and stop fretting about what you *cannot* do—or using that as an excuse for laziness.

Fact. Exercise *matters*!

> **If you aim to be healthy from head to toe,**
> **Exercise helps keep you in the know.**
> **It's one of the very best things you can do**
> **For brain, body, and immune system, too.**

"I'm going to brain-stimulation class," barked Barkowitz. "Wanna come along?"

"Now why ever would I do that?" growled Woofgang. "I could teach that class myself!"

"Maybe," barked Barkowitz. "On the other hand, you might learn something new... Hey, what's with your eyes bugging out of their sockets?"

"Dunno, for sure," growled Woofgang. "I do know things are a bit blurry and my head aches."

"Well, I suppose you were wise enough to check with the doctor," barked Barkowitz.

"The office gave me new glasses but they didn't help," growled Woofgang. "Charlatans—all!"

"I say, what's that flashy thing around your neck?" barked Barkowitz. "A treatment?"

"What do you think it is?" growled Woofgang. "My new collar, of course. Cost two paws and a tail for all those fancy Dawgstones. My collar is the envy of everyone! Now, be off with you."

"Sure you won't come?" barked Barkowitz.

"Naw. All I need to know I already learned in Pupgarten," growled Woofgang.

Not everything, thought Barkowitz. *That collar is way too small for your neck...no wonder your eyes are bugging out. That can't be good!*

5—Brain Stimulation

Fact. Although it is not a muscle, the brain responds much the same as muscle tissue. According to Richard Restak, MD, physical exercise (the single *most powerful* tool to optimize your brain function) can improve creativity, concentration, problem-solving, and help delay the onset of any memory loss. It prepares your neurons to connect with each other, while mental stimulation allows your brain to capitalize on that readiness.

Fact. Much as the body craves food and physical activity, your brain craves information, variety, and novelty. Brain stimulation is essential for every brain and critical for the aging brain, which has a bent towards mental laziness. Avoid zoning out in front of the TV, letting your brain passively process what another brain created. Instead, maximize active mental picturing by engaging in stimulating and challenging mental activities for at least 30 minutes a day to keep your brain active and your axons and dendrites stretched out.

Fact. Individuals who are aerobically fit may also have an intellectual edge. Metaphorically, picture your hand as a neuron. Your palm is the cell body. Your thumb is the axon, the highway by which information leaves the cell and goes to another neuron. Your fingers are the dendrites that receive information and pull it into the cell. Studies have shown that dendrites can alter their shape in 30 seconds and a neuron can grow a new dendrite in 30 minutes—depending on the amount of stimulation the neurons receive. It is possible to grow 10,000 dendritic fingerlike projections (or more) on each neuron that can, in turn, connect with other neurons.

Fact. If not stimulated on a regular basis, neurons—along with their axons and dendrites—can atrophy, or shrink. This widens the synapse (space) between neurons, making the transfer of information from one neuron to another more difficult. Eventually, brain tissue itself can begin to shrink and pull away from the skull. Imagine a neuron that receives low levels of stimulation looking something like a tree in winter with bare branches and no leaves. Next, picture a neuron that receives challenging mental stimulation on a regular basis now looking like a fully leafed-out tree. Big difference. Which does *your* brain want?

Fact. There are many ways to "use it"—brain aerobics, if you will—in order to retain optimum brain function for as long as possible. The following are a few suggestions to get you started:

- Play mental and word games. Some like to access games on lumosity.com *or* Posit Science *or* www.ArleneTaylor.org

- Read *aloud* for ten minutes a day to promote more brain-function activity and language development—in both children and adults. Listen to audio books. Hone your creativity in every way possible!

- Travel (locally, nationally, internationally) can expose your brain to new sights, sounds, smells, tastes, people, and environments.

- If you play an instrument, keep practicing on a regular basis. If not, it's never too late to learn.

- Develop a challenging and rewarding hobby. Volunteer in a genre that interests you. Learn to use a computer and do Internet searches. Make your life a treasured treasure hunt.

Fact. Brain + Body = an amazing team. But you get only one of each in life's big scheme. *Use* it or *lose* it—know that right up front. A healthy body without a healthy brain is less than half the picture—and vice versa. Give your brain mental challenges.

Fact. Brain stimulation *matters!*

You brain's not a muscle, yet it acts like one.
Use it or lose it when all's said and done.
Read aloud ten minutes—challenge your mind.
Prevent your memory from lagging behind.

"You seem a tad out of sorts this fine morning," chirruped Kingfisher. "A bit cantankerous, if I may say so. Not that it's any of my business, you understand—but I just couldn't help noticing."

"Hey, I am starving, don't you know!" Flycatcher sputtered irritably. "If you'd been up all night trying to catch a snack—without success—you'd be crotchety, too. Don't know where all those infernal insects disappeared to . . ."

"Methinks you've been losing sleep again," chirruped Kingfisher. "If you want to be around a long time to keep catching snacks, you'd best shut your eyes when the sun goes down. First thing in the morning you'll likely catch plenty."

"And since when did you become my personal coach?" demanded Flycatcher, testily. "Did I ask for any suggestions? Did I? Did I?"

"Just saying," chirruped Kingfisher, mildly. "What are friends for? Lose sleep, shorten your life. It's that simple. Naturally your choice, of course. But I'd like to see you around for a while. So, if I were you ..."

"Well, you're not!" snapped Flycatcher. "And don't you forget it!"

And I thank my lucky stars for that, thought Kingfisher to himself.

6—Optimum Sleep

Fact. All living creatures on Planet Earth need sleep during each 24-hour period. Sleep may be more essential than food, since animals will die from sleep deprivation sooner than from starvation. Your brain does not *rest* during sleep per se, since hundreds of biological processes continue. Some brain areas are even more active when asleep than when awake, due to their many housekeeping chores that typically require 7-8 hours to accomplish for most adults. Imagine hiring a cleaning service where the workers routinely leave an hour or two before their shift is over. As they continue to cut their work time short, it doesn't take long for "unfinished tasks" to accumulate. Soon the workers are too far behind to catch up!

Fact. Sleep deprivation is pandemic: an estimated 80 percent of the world's population needs an alarm clock to wake up. Estimates are that 80 million Americans are sleep deprived, meaning their brains are not getting the optimum sleep needed to accomplish required functions. A contributing factor likely relates to the invention of electric lights, which can cause a mismatch between biology and technology.

Fact. During sleep, human growth hormones are produced. Electricity is generated for thinking and energy production. Hormones, neurotransmitters, enzymes, and other chemicals are replenished. Neurotrophins (food for the neurons) are created, cells repaired, the immune system strengthened, and metabolic wastes excreted. During sleep, the brain can experiment without inhibition, often coming up with never-before-imagined ideas. Sufficient sleep lowers the risk for dementia, depression, psychosis, and stroke. Lack of sleep can drain brain-body energy, interfere with effective decision-making and problem-solving, increase the risk for mistakes and accidents, trigger weight gain, increase irritability, and accelerate the aging process.

Fact. All cognitive memory functions are impacted in some way by sleep deprivation. This includes declarative (semantic and episodic) memory, along with implicit (non-declarative) memory, and intelligent or creative memory. Sleep is essential for all healthy memory functions. When awake and exposed to new information, the brain shoves what it learns into short-term memory banks. During sleep, the brain consolidates the information. Think of the hippocampus (the brain's "search engine") as rewinding and replaying what happened during the day for the neocortex or cerebrum to review. During this process, information is either discarded or moved into long-term storage. When you consciously want to retrieve a memory, the hippocampus searches for and (hopefully) locates the information—if having been moved into long-term memory. Unfortunately, lack of sufficient sleep will interfere with all types of memory functions.

Fact. Melatonin is a hormone that impacts sleep and helps regulate biological rhythms. Light from any source slows the release of melatonin from the pineal gland. Sleeping in a dark room can help avoid interfering with melatonin production, as can removing all electronic products from the bedroom. An hour before bedtime, turn off all blue-light-emitting diodes or LEDs (unless you have been wearing special glasses that block the blue light from entering your eyes), as these suppress melatonin production and increase alertness—exactly what you do *not* want when you need sleep.

Fact. Sleep is independently linked with longevity. Without enough sleep, you die. The loss of one hour of sleep per night can shorten your life span. Sleep has been called the "golden chain" that ties your health and body together. Give your brain and body the *optimum* amount of sleep they need.

Fact. Sleep *matters!*

While you sleep, your brain does its chores,
As energy, memory, and joy it restores.
You pay a stiff price when you try to cheat
On sleep—as brain function can deplete.

"My but I have a nasty headache," barked Hyena grumpily.

"Not again!" said friend, Camel. "That's  twice this week!"

"I know that," barked Hyena. "I can count. I'm not stupid. I just have a right nasty headache."

"I do not recall any remarks about *stupid,*" commented Camel, placidly. "I do notice a rather high level of irritability." Hyena completely ignored Camel's observation.

"Have you been to the water hole and sucked up a stomach full of liquid refreshment yet today?" asked Camel. "Headache and irritability are two common symptoms of dehydration…"

"I'm not thirsty," barked Hyena. "I told you, I just have a right nasty headache."

"So I heard," said Camel. "At a one percent level of dehydration, your brain has a five percent drop in cognitive ability—and that may be long before you experience any thirst sensation."

"You may have a point," said Hyena. "I cleaned up left-overs this morning instead of going to the water hole. Think I'll trot down there now."

"I knew you had a brain," said Camel. "I'll go along and get a fill-up myself. Then we can head over to the oasis and see what's happening. Maybe catch a few winks in a spot of shade…"

7—Essential Hydration

Fact. Many have learned to survive without love. None without water! Dehydration from water deprivation kills faster than the lack of any other nutrient. You can live at least ten times longer without food than without water. Similar to estimates of the composition of Planet Earth, body and brain average about 75 percent water and 25 percent solid matter. However, brain cells themselves are closer to 86 percent water; blood, around 83 percent. Dehydration represents an alteration in this ratio toward more solid matter.

Fact. Water is your most essential nutrient—next to oxygen. The price of dehydration's price is high, impacting *all* brain-body systems but especially lethal to brain function, slowing it down and interfering with vital thinking processes. A *one* percent level of dehydration results in a *five* percent reduction in cognitive ability—and you probably aren't even feeling thirsty yet! A cognitive reduction may lead to difficulties making change while shopping, navigating around town, or deciding between two options.

Fact. Normally, there is more water inside a cell than outside. Dehydration reverses that ratio. Water generates the electrical energy for *all* brain functions. In fact, the movement of water in and out of the cells functions much like a hydroelectric plant. Brain cells need at least twice the energy required by most other cells in the body and three times that required by muscle tissue. Water provides this energy more effectively than any other substance. When water levels fall, energy production also falls.

Fact. Dehydration can cause brain tissue to shrink and pull away from the skull, a condition now linked with dementia. It is also associated with lymph fluid problems and low blood volume, increased risk of clotting, headaches, irritability, inflammation, kidney failure, heat cramps, heatstroke, depression, and seizures due to electrolyte loss. Dehydration produces free radicals that wrinkle the skin, as well as internal body organs. Unpleasant thought, that.

Fact. Many children grow up being given food when they are fussy instead of first being offered water to determine if they are just thirsty—or physiologically hungry. Consequently, many never learn to differentiate between genuine physiological hunger and thirst. In addition, because thirst sensation tends to fall with age, it is not a reliable indicator of dehydration. Fifteen to thirty minutes before a meal, drink a glass of water to ensure you are eating from hunger rather than from thirst. The water can also increase the fluidity of digestive juices and help them handle the food you've eaten more efficiently.

Fact. Estimates are that most people over the age of 50 drink less than 1 quart (32 oz.) or 1 liter (1,000 ml) of water per day. The average adult loses more than 80 oz. (2365 ml) of water daily through sweating, breathing, and waste elimination, which puts the individual 48 ounces (1420 ml) in deficit compared to the amount of water taken in. Studies have shown that some children *and* adults drink mostly sodas (regular or diet), fruit juices, sugary drinks, tea, coffee, or colas. According to Dr. Corinne Allen, founder of Advanced Learning & Development Institute, those with brain challenges (such as head injuries, anxiety, depression, the autism spectrum, or ADD/ADHD) often drink little (if any) water each day. The resulting dehydration can exacerbates the brain's dysfunction.

Fact. Body organs will sacrifice their need for water in favor of the brain. Avoid *that*. Unless medically contraindicated, drink enough pure water for one or two pale urines daily. Both your brain and body will thank you. According to basketball star Stephen Curry, water is "essential" to a healthy lifestyle. Some say water is your first and foremost *medicine.*

Fact. Water *matters!*

The nutrient water is quintessential;
An insufficiency is consequential.
Dehydration derails cognition,
Leaving your brain in a dreadful condition!

"He landed on his head, you say?" asked Flighty. "On his head? How could that possibly happen? He's got wings, for bird's sake!"

"Oh, it gets worse," said the reporter, rising to the occasion and fluffing out chest feathers. "Much worse. First, he overate and got punch-drunk on those red berries. Stupid choice! Then at some point he tried demonstrating his version of bird-brain prancing on a top branch in that tall tree over yonder—and miscalculated badly!"

"Punch drunk!" exclaimed Flighty. "He knows better than to eat those berries! Almost every time he does, something dastardly happens!"

"The operative word here may be 'should have known' and not *knows*. You realize it's a very long way down to that rocky ledge," continued the reporter, "and he was so spifflicated he didn't even spread his wings, poor fella. Smashed his skull but good, he did. Feathers flying around like shooting stars. Naturally, his folks are very near to being inconsolable."

"Yikes! That must have hurt," said Flighty.

"Well, it was definitely more than an 'owie!' But hey, there's always a silver lining," the reporter said, yawning. "His college fund will now cover the cost of the rehabilitation center."

And here I thought humans were the only ones with such poor judgement, thought Flighty.

8—Brain-Body Safety

Fact. You only have one brain. No replacement is available, so it's prevention all the way. You only have one body, as well. While some body-organ replacements exist, they are often less efficient. Safety is important for both the brain and body since (as Thomas Edison put it) the chief function of your body is to carry around your brain. A functional brain in a diseased or damaged body can often accomplish a great deal. But a damaged or diseased brain in an otherwise functional body? Not so much.

Fact. Your neurons (thinking cells) typically do not replace themselves by dividing and multiplying as do most other body cells. Therefore, your brain's neurons today are the same your brain had at birth. Guard them! Safety includes paying attention to the researched strategies related to health and longevity of these vital cells in *both* your brain and body.

Fact. Broken bones, head injuries, sexually-transmitted diseases, and many addictive behaviors can cut short a life that might have lived and thrived successfully for another decade or two, never mind a life-time. Be proactive about safety on a daily basis. *Knowing* is one thing; *implementing* what you know is another. While genuine accidents do occur, prevention—which isn't rocket science—can be very helpful. Many simple prevention strategies have been identified. For example:

- As far as possible, avoid exposure to radiation, toxins, poisons, substances known to be harmful to brain or body, and transmissible infectious diseases.

- Protect your mind. Avoid exposing it to negative pictures, images, or ideas that might return to disturb sleep or trigger undesirable behaviors resulting in injury or death.

- Protect your lungs: inhale fresh air, minimize exposure to pollutants such as tobacco smoke, side-smoke, vehicle exhaust, and fire smoke. Wear a mask if air quality is poor.

- Protect your ears when around loud sounds. Protect your eyes when involved in activities that could trigger flying debris.

- Protect your digestive system from low-quality foods and beverages--*anything* that could diminish its effectiveness.

- Avoid substances that may negatively damage the brain's neuronal control centers. Minimize the use of alcoholic beverages. If you choose to drink, do not drive!

- Fall-proof your home. Remove throw rugs and other tripping hazards. Use sturdy step-stools when reaching for high objects. Be careful with ladders--and stay off the roof. (Leave those activities to the experts!)

- Protect your head. Wear a helmet when bike riding or engaging in any activity that has a higher risk of head injuries. At all cost, take care to avoid concussions and skull fractures whenever possible.

- Avoid distracted walking and driving. Wear seatbelts when in vehicles. (You know the drill!)

Fact. The first time you do something, your brain lays out the outline of new software in case you want to do it again. The good news is that this makes repeating that something easier. The bad news is that the brain can end up developing some pretty deleterious habits because you "did something once." Some less-well-informed daredevil may be willing to risk life and limb but that doesn't mean you want or need to. Think ahead. Make good decisions about what you choose to do *once*.

Fact. Safety *matters!*

> **Life has a myriad things you can do,**
> **But you have no wings, so get a clue.**
> **You can be wise and still have a blast—**
> **Creating a future and not just a past.**

"Hello! Kreepie? What are you doing out there on the trail in the heat of the day?" asked Crawley.

"What does it look like?" asked Kreepie.

"Like you're letting the sun crisp your shell, that's what," said Crawley.

"I suppose it's just possible that I may be in a spot of trouble," Kreepie replied, slowly.

"Ya *think*? What was your first clue?" retorted Crawley. "I'd have thought a gastropod definitely would have known better."

"Well, Pa did suggest I wait 'til the cool of the evening, but hey, he's no rocket scientist, so I blew him off. That may have been a small error in snail judgement." Kreepie sighed.

"A bit late to conclude that," said Crawley. "*My* Pa says no snail can know everything, so we each need a few snails we can trust—to give us feedback, don't you know."

"All I know is that I'm as dry as those hills of Gilboa, wherever they are; so dry, in fact, I have no slime to slide on whatsoever," said Kreepie. "Got any bright ideas?"

"I wish I did!" Crawley replied. "I'd like to help, I really would, but even if it were safe to join you, you know there's no way to share snail slime. You better start hoping it rains—and soon!"

9—Sunlight

Fact. Life cannot survive on this planet—much less thrive—without some exposure to natural sunlight. But how and when you get it—plus the amount—can be critical. Debates continue about how much sunlight is optimum, although avoiding sunburn is *not* up for debate. Exposing one's arms to natural light for an estimated 10-15 minutes a day can provide the needed benefits. (Dark skin may need five or six times that amount.) Of course, there is no one-size-fits-all. *Excessive* can be defined as inappropriate amounts of exposure to the sun's ultraviolet radiation (UVR) for your skin type.

Fact. Beyond the known effects related to Vitamin D production and calcium utilization, sunlight turns on internal chemical reactions and stimulates enzymes to work more effectively. Brain plasticity and depression, regulated in part by Brain-Derived Neurotrophic Factor (BDNF), show a correlation with the amount of ambient sunlight.

Fact. The suprachiasmatic nucleus (SCN), a group of cells in the brain's hypothalamus, uses signals from the eyes to keep the human circadian rhythm in sync with the sun—resetting the brain's 24-hour biological clock on a regular basis. Known as *entrainment,* this process occurs when light-sensitive cells in the retina send electrical signals to the SCN. If natural light cannot get to the retina, the cycle of the circadian clock begins to lengthen beyond the usual 24-hours and a few minutes, which can be disruptive to a person's life. In the morning, as sunlight enters the eyes, the SCN is activated and wakes up the body organs, notifying the pineal gland to stop secreting melatonin. At sundown, the SCN tells the pineal gland to release the hormone melatonin, which helps to promote a sense of being sleepy. Exposing the brain to artificial light after sundown can interrupt the release of melatonin.

Fact. Jet lag puts the brain in conflict with a person's normal sleep patterns, as the brain scrambles to adjust to crossing many different time zones. For some, this can take a day for every time zone crossed, often causing problems with effective thinking and efficient performance. Similar symptoms can occur when a person works rotating shifts or when sleep times differ radically on weekends and the brain tries to adapt to shorter, longer, or irregular hours.

Fact. Some teenagers can experience a sleep-phase delay. Because their melatonin levels naturally rise later at night (compared with many children and adults) adolescents feel alert later, making it difficult to fall asleep before eleven o'clock—or even midnight. Sleep deprivation, compounded by early school start-times, can negatively influence *life* in general and *learning* in particular. Keeping lights dim as bedtime approaches, turning off electronics an hour before bedtime (or wearing special glasses to block LED light), along with exposure to bright light as soon as possible in the morning may be helpful.

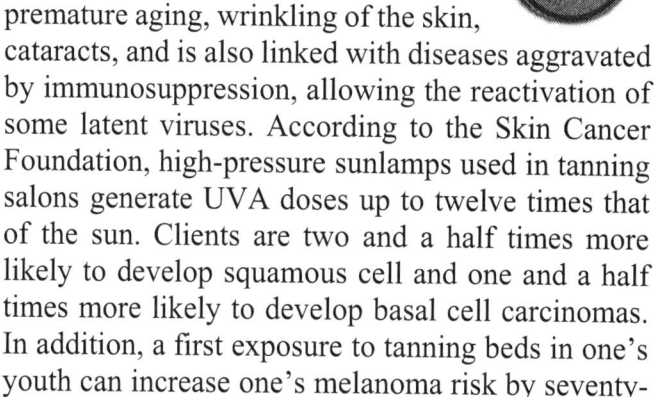

Fact. Excessive and unprotected exposure to sunlight can contribute to premature aging, wrinkling of the skin, cataracts, and is also linked with diseases aggravated by immunosuppression, allowing the reactivation of some latent viruses. According to the Skin Cancer Foundation, high-pressure sunlamps used in tanning salons generate UVA doses up to twelve times that of the sun. Clients are two and a half times more likely to develop squamous cell and one and a half times more likely to develop basal cell carcinomas. In addition, a first exposure to tanning beds in one's youth can increase one's melanoma risk by seventy-five percent.

Fact. Exposure to the ultraviolet radiation in sunlight has both beneficial and deleterious effects. Too little is bad: so is too much. Flood your home with sunlight, but be prudent about your own exposure.

Fact. Sunshine exposure *matters!*

The sun bathes earth with warming light,
And keeps your brain-clock working right.
By night the moon takes on its glow
As light for all who come and go.

"Just finished a new verse," said Raven, in his deep, throaty Kraa. "I saw it happen, myself."

"Saw what happen?" asked Noir.

"I just told you. What I saw yesterday and what I wrote about in my new verse," said Raven.

"Okay, lay it on me," said Noir, with a big raven sigh. "I am pretty sure you want me to listen."

> Icky Gooey was a snail,
> And thus begins this terrible tale.
> It was a snail a bit headstrong,
> That made a choice so deadly wrong.
> Alone it slid the railroad track,
> Then stopped, distracted with a snack.
> Of course, the train it did not see,
> On that account all do agree.
> And as the train bore down full sail,
> That snail was melded to the rail.
> All in all 'twas very sad.
> Icky Gooey's gone, too bad.

"Hey, sad story and all, but the verse is close to decent," said Noir. "How in the name of black feathers does your brain think up that stuff?"

"From you, that's high praise," said Raven, his gravelly Kraa rumbling. "I eat right, don't you know. I feed *my* brain high-quality food!"

"Hmm-m. Can we chat about that over lunch?" asked Noir. "I have an idea for a new song . . ."

10—Nutrition

**Fact.** In the long term, dieting doesn't work. Period. Short term, dieting—especially fad and radical—*can* result in the loss of a few pounds, but within about three years most people gain it all (or more) back, often as fat rather than muscle tissue. Also of potential concern, experiments with mice at the Albert Einstein College of Medicine show that when neurons are starved, these nutrition-hungry brain cells actually begin to eat parts of themselves in an attempt to send out hunger distress signals.

Fact. Although the body can use proteins, fats, *or* carbohydrates for energy, brain cells reportedly prefer glucose from carbs almost *exclusively* as a source of energy. Due to rapid metabolism—levels fall during periods of intense cognitive processing—the brain requires minute-to-minute glucose. Studies on all types of people have shown improved mental ability after a meal high in carbs, which raises concerns about the long-term impact on the brain from "low-carb" dieting Preferred are healthier complex carbs (relatively low on the Glycemic Index and Glycemic Load lists), eaten in as natural a state as possible. High-sugar foods and beverages can trigger a glucose spike in the brain, usually followed by a dramatic low. Much like a roller-coaster, this fluctuating pattern of glucose highs and lows can be *deadly* for many brain functions while also causing low-grade inflammation.

Fact. Calories from low-quality foods and beverages will likely go to your *waist.* (What a *waste!*) In addition, aromatase in fat cells converts testosterone into estrogen, which can cause a plethora of problems in both males and females—problems no one wants. *Avoid* overeating, especially of poor quality foods—such as those high in animal fat or hydrogenated oils or sugar. *Minimize* highly refined and processed foods which can trigger hormonal imbalances and increase a risk of insulin resistance, visceral fat accumulation, and type 2 diabetes. *Increase* your intake of soluble and insoluble fiber, preferably from whole, intact foods.

Fact. Prudent "intermittent fasting" has been shown to enhance cardiovascular function, sleep, digestion, cell repair, and weight management. It can also reduce the risk of inflammation, believed to underlie many types of illnesses, disease, and the process of aging. For example, if you eat breakfast at 8:00 a.m., lunch at noon, and your last meal before 6:00 p.m.—and drink only water between then and "break-fast" the next morning—you will have fasted for 13-14 hours. Alternatively, some choose to eat just two meals a day on weekends or skip dinner altogether once or twice a week. If you try this, select a wise option that works for your brain, body, and schedule, carefully avoiding excess fasting.

Fact. Both brain and body perform most effectively with appropriate amounts of high-quality nutrition. Be wise to energize! Consider these tips:

- Read labels carefully and avoid high-sugar, high-salt, high-fat, and additives ending in -*ate*.
- Move toward a Mediterranean-style cuisine of plant-based, unrefined, and unprocessed foods.
- Practice appropriate portion control.
- Avoid colas (regular or diet), fruit juices, and sugary drinks. Minimize alcohol intake.
- Rotate bites of food to maintain flavor intensity. If you choose dessert, eat only two or three bites. After that, you're eating primarily from taste-bud memory anyway.
- Avoid *empty* calories and choose *nutritious* ones; minimize *chew-less* foods in favor of *chewy* ones; dump *snacking* and implement *regular* mealtimes.
- Make water your "beverage of choice," as it is absorbed quickly and needs no digestion. Drink a glass of water 15-30 minutes before each meal.

Fact. Quality nutrition *matters*!

Use food as medicine to help you thrive,
Choose well and avoid a low-glucose dive.
Dump "live to eat"—instead "eat to live"—
A Longevity Lifestyle that is preventive.

LLM—Just the Facts!

"What's all that stuff going on down yonder?" asked little Kooka.

"Just a humanoid, recording," said Big Burra, with a characteristic laugh.

"Recording what?" persisted Kooka.

"Probably background sounds for another jungle movie," retorted Big Burra. "Our laughter was used in the Tarzan movies in the 1930s and even in The Lost World: Jurassic Park."

"Wow! Do we get royalties?" asked little Kooka.

"Royalties?" asked Big Burra, with a burst of laughter, so catching that Kooka joined in. "Royalties? You bet! Our 'royalties' are living longer and healthier than most birds or humanoids because we *laugh* a lot!"

"Do humanoids laugh?" asked little Kooka. "I've never heard one laugh really mirthfully."

Some do," said Big Burra. "Many don't. That's part of the reason they die so young. "They'd rather whine, complain, argue, and gossip."

"Let's get the family together and let that humanoid record what a really good laugh session sounds like," said little Kooka, excitedly. "I'd like to be in a jungle movie, I would!"

And that's exactly what they did!

11—Laughter

 **Fact.** Mirthful laughter is a miracle medicine, requiring no visits to healthcare professionals or prescriptions, no special outfit or environment. Think of laughter as a form of play—for *both* your brain and body—while also being very beneficial. An interesting phenomenon, laughter is considered a form of audible speech, arising from Broca's Area in the brain's left frontal lobe. Indeed, you can convey much through laughter: anger, fear, sadness, scorn, derision, or joy, happiness, affirmation, and so on.

Fact. Humor, a mental faculty located in the right cerebral hemisphere, typically activates when something you did not expect to see, hear, or think occurs. *If* you have honed your sense of humor, that is. Humor may be triggered by seeing a person skid unexpectedly on a banana peel or from hearing a child make unusual sounds. The identified humor can then trigger laughter. Not everyone chooses to laugh, however. As opposed to sustained and mirthful laughter, a verbal acknowledgement that something is funny does not appear to trigger the same release of feel-better chemicals.

Fact. Much like yawning, laughter is an intensely infectious activity that triggers the Brain Reward System. Dr. Madan Kataria of India found that when groups of individuals get together and *choose* to laugh, before long it becomes genuine laughter. Brief humor-related laughter comes from the brain. *Choosing to laugh* disengages you from regular life, which may not be very humorous at the moment. Laughing from your diaphragm helps rid the lungs of residual air and makes room for deep inhalations of fresh air. When sustained laughter comes from the inside, the brain *gets* it and releases endorphins, dopamine, and serotonin to help you feel better.

Fact. Laughter can be *reflexive.* It is virtually impossible to control laughter when you are being tickled playfully—something you can't accomplish alone. (You're in control when tickling yourself and there's no surprise!) Laughter can also be *instinctual,* as in hearing the unexpected punchline on a joke. Instinctual laughter appears to be linked with your brain's overseer, the hypothalamus. You may or may not be able to control instinctual laughter, especially if you're being told to "stop laughing." *Good luck*!

Fact. Perception differences of what is "funny" typically exist between males and females. Female humor tends toward word play in the left hemisphere and stories about something that strikes a woman's funny bone. Females connect through language, but not necessarily through jokes. Male humor is more right-brained; they use jokes to connect or slapstick humor requiring no language. Learning each other's humor *is* possible—and doubles one's triggers for laughter. Some universities now offer courses in understanding male-female humor. Studies show that humor and laughter promote healthier relationships: couples who laugh together tend to stay together! After all, who can hold onto anger or hurt while doubled over in mirthful laughter?

Fact. Studies suggest getting at least 30 mirthful laughs a day for good health. People judged to be "very happy" reportedly laugh from 100-400 times a day. And children? 400-600 times a day—unless their laughter is stifled by being told to "Stop being silly. Grow up!" (They will, all too soon.) Be serious about life but avoid taking every little thing *too* seriously. Approach life as an important—but fun!— experience where you look for and purposely schedule opportunities to laugh. Hone your sense of humor—it's a skill! Expand what your brain finds funny. Need help? Join a laugh club. Hang out with people who have a great sense of humor. Learn to laugh at yourself. Don't feel like laughing right now? Choose to do it anyway and keep at it. Mirthful laughter *is* a miracle medicine. (Perhaps the best!) And a cheerful mind works healing. Laugh and *last*.

Fact. Sustained mirthful laughter *matters!*

A spoonful of laughter is great medicine,
A personal spacecraft, a magic spin,
That whisks you away anywhere anytime,
And returns you with a new paradigm.

"Of course I'm going alone," said Black Bird. "Most of this murder of crows are boring—even dumb. Don't want to be around 'em."

"A few," conceded his uncle. "Hardly most. This gusty wind could tumble you against a rock in a nano-second—and we'd never find you." Black Bird shrugged his feathers and took flight.

"I say," squawked Ebony, landing on the edge of a small crevice. "Graywing and I have been out searching for your black feathers for two days!

"I'm history" said Black Bird, surprised. "Wasted effort. My foot is bruised … can't climb out."

"Mind your head," cawed Ebony. "We'll drop pebbles over the edge. Just keep stepping up."

"Not such a dumb idea," thought Black Bird, again surprised, as pebbles rained into the crevice. "Ah, thanks. I doubt my brain would have thought of this brilliant solution."

"Well, no one crow can think of everything," said Ebony as they took wing.

One day when Black Bird no longer hopped lopsidedly around like a drunken sailor, Ebony swooped in. "Got an idea for a new game. Any chance you'd like to collaborate?
Your choice, of course."

Black Bird would.

12—Support System

Fact. In the winter of 1624 and while seriously ill, John Donne wrote a famous poem in which he opined that no one is an island, each is a piece of the continent. Each human being needs a few individuals who "have your back." Since you are the only person who will be with you for your entire life, your relationship with yourself is of paramount importance. Equally so, that small circle of genuine and trusted friends with whom you feel free to share joys, hopes, and puzzlements as needed. They may be biological-family or family-of-choice. Those with a good support system tend to be healthier and live longer than those who don't. In one survey, the average female identified nine people to whom she could easily relate. The average male identified either one or none. If one, he typically named his spouse. No wonder divorce can be so emotionally devastating to a male: he loses his one support person.

Fact. The people you hang out with matter! According to Jim Rohn, you are the average of the four or five people with whom you spend the most time. According to study estimates, within three years you are at risk for picking up their habits, especially those related to happiness, smoking, health, and obesity. Greek Philosopher Epictetus believed that the key is to keep company only with those who uplift you, whose presence calls forth your best. Your close friends can enhance or sabotage your success. Surround yourself with those who:

- Exhibit a healthy superego and practice meaningful and consistent self-care
- Create and maintain a positive mindset and effective self-talk patterns
- Sa good sense of humor—and laugh *a lot*
- Are wise and supportive, making healthier choices with the future in mind
- Study, learn, turn information into knowledge, and apply it on a daily basis
- Embrace a Longevity Lifestyle

Fact. As water seeks its own level, so do brains and behaviors. Identify the type of individual you want to have around *you*—then become that person yourself. As you grow, you will more naturally be attracted *by* and become attractive *to* those who are on a similar life journey. These then become the type of individual you want for your support system. In turn, you may be able to do that for one or more of them.

Fact. A support system is about relationships, which take some work and commitment. However, giving and receiving is a tricky equation. It's not that you are keeping score, per se, but relationships in a support system need to be reciprocal—never a one-way street in giving or taking. Sometimes you give;

sometimes you receive. Those with an overinflated sense of self-worth are often comfortable taking but not giving. Others with an underinflated sense often give—endlessly, at times—but are uncomfortable receiving. That equation needs to be in balance. If you lean toward either extreme on that continuum, you may have some work to do. When someone wants to give and you dismiss their efforts—either because you feel unworthy or have an issue with never wanting to owe anyone anything—you deprive them of the opportunity to feel good about what they were able to do for or with you. This could be viewed as a selfish or self-centered choice on your part.

Fact. The value of relationships with those you love and who love you—your *support system*, in effect—is inestimable. Many have said they most regret not what they *did* but what they did *not* do, the friendship opportunities they failed to appreciate and nurture—until too late. Select the members of your support system with great care, as well as the ones with which you choose to engage. Do both wisely, keeping your life in balance. Remember, genuine love is the only thing that is everything.

Fact. A support system *matters!*

No one is an island and each has a skill—
Though all require help on a very steep hill.
Don't need an army, just a few tried and true,
Willing to help out—impromptu.

"Hey there, Sis," said Water-rat, cheerfully. "Isn't a wonderful day, don't you know!"

"Not for me. I am so-o-o-o stressed—big time! Rudy-Rat's behaviors are driving me nuts."

"His behaviors are not the problem. He's just using them to manage underlying problems he's ignored for years," said Water-rat.

"I'm not blame-free, either, you know. I feel sorry for myself and shop to feel better. He gets mad that we're in debt and acts out. I feel sorry for myself and shop … I'm running on an endless treadmill and going absolutely nowhere."

"Oh, you're definitely going somewhere," said Water-rat. "Downhill, I might add."

"Guess I don't know how to get off this infernal exercise wheel," said his sister.

"If you keep doing what you're doing you'll keep getting what you're getting. Change the way you think and change the way you manage stressors!" said Water-rat. "But you can only do it for you."

"So how would I start?" asked his sister.

"Come to stress class with me—whenever you're ready, that is. No pressure! Just remember that everyone needs help now and again."

"Stress class you say? Hey, I'm ready *now*! Let's go-o-o-o! What are we waiting for?"

13—Stressor Management

Fact. János Hugo Bruno "Hans" Selye (1907-1982), a pioneering Hungarian-Canadian endocrinologist, was reportedly the first to demonstrate the existence of physical, mental, and emotional responses by a biological organism to a stimulus. Eventually, Dr. Selye borrowed the descriptive word *stress* from the field of engineering and applied it to human beings. Stress responses are generally learned in childhood, typically from observing how the "big people" in your life behave and function—especially during stressful situations. The goal is to embrace *Eustress* (positive stress that helps you grow) while minimizing *Distress* (negative stress) and *Misstress* (hidden negative stress). Unmanaged distress and misstress can damage body organs, increase risk of disease, ruin relationships, kill brain cells, and even result in a shortened lifespan.

Fact. Stress can be triggered by external and/or internal factors. According to Dr. Al Seibert, no stress exists in any situation unless an individual human brain perceives something as a stressor and experiences strain. The *stress* is less the result of what actually occurs or exists objectively and far more because of the way in which the brain perceives what is happening. This means that stress is as unique as both your fingerprints and your brain. Its subjectivity is reminiscent of an old proverb: *One person's pleasure is another person's pain.*

Fact. Epictetus, a freed slave and 2nd century Greek philosopher, taught that it isn't so much what happens to you that matters but what you *think* about what happens. This is sometimes referred to as a "20:80 Rule." Only twenty percent of any negative impact to your brain and body is due to the identified stressor. At least *eighty* percent is due to your perception of the stressor and how much weight or importance you choose to give it. Here's the bottom line: while you may not be able to prevent the twenty percent in any given situation, you *can* do everything about the eighty percent—because your *brain* creates your own personal perceptions.

Fact. Managing distress and misstress effectively relates to both perception and flexibility. As you have seen, trees that cannot flex with the wind are at high risk of being uprooted in a storm. The same with human beings. It is estimated that fully half of the stressors humans grapple with are of their own making based on how they think. Your perception of the stressor, learned reactions, degree of flexibility, level of emotional intelligence, ability to be serious about life (while not taking every little thing *too* seriously), along with acquired "tools and strategies," all influence the stressor's impact and the results you experience in both your brain and body, and often in your relationships, as well.

Fact. "Reframing" can be a helpful stress-management strategy. Changing the frame on a painting can alter the way it looks—sometimes rather dramatically. Try viewing a perceived stressor in a new light, perhaps imagining how a complete stranger might see it. Or you might try not only perceiving but responding in a totally different way, and *a change may be as good as a rest.* Sometimes this is enough to help you brainstorm a workable solution. Ask yourself: "Will this event or situation (*stressor*) matter in twelve months?" If *yes*, do the work to brainstorm and problem-solve. If *no*, just let it go!

Fact. Many react to perceived stressors using beliefs and attitudes that were absorbed before the age of six. Examine your triggers, stress patterns, personal perceptions, learned reactions, exhibited behaviors, *and* their consequences. If your stressor strategies are resulting in negative outcomes, craft and implement healthier responses. Thank your brain for helping you make choices and exhibit behaviors that result in more positive outcomes. Live the 20:80 Rule on a daily basis—not just when a stressor strikes.

Fact. Stressor management *matters!*

> **Stressors can make life a slippery slope,**
> **But with some thought you can find new hope.**
> **The 20:80 Rule can help get you through.**
> **Reframe, use EQ—there's a lot you can do.**

"Is there some reason you are out here devouring every insect you can wrap your tongue around?" asked Gecko. "You can't be all that hungry and these are rather low on the gourmet scale."

"Well," drawled his cousin, Gekey, "our fine-Feathered friend on yonder branch can't get to sleep because of these pesky insects."

"You'll never eat 'em all, you know," said Gecko "You are only one, for lizard's sake!"

"I know," replied Gekey, "but I am *one*. And I can put away quite a few of 'em. Insects are not entirely stupid. Look, they're already starting to change direction as their buddies disappear."

"And what difference did all of your efforts make, I ask you?" persisted Gecko.

"It made a difference for our fine feathered friend," replied Gekey. "Look, he just tucked his head under a wing. Let's be perfectly honest; *his* tongue is completely useless for this job!"

"Well, as long as I'm already here, I may as well pitch in and help," said Gecko, sighing. "Couldn't hurt, good source of protein and all. Might even make my life a bit more interesting."

"A random act of kindness always gives me a new sense of satisfaction," said Gekey. There was no response. Gecko's tongue was very busy…

14—Life Satisfaction

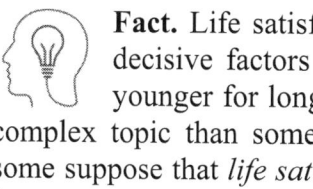**Fact.** Life satisfaction is one of the most decisive factors for staying healthier and younger for longer. However, it is a more complex topic than some might realize. Although some suppose that *life satisfaction* is a synonym for *happiness*, life satisfaction represents a separate concept. It is the evaluation of one's life as a whole, rather than just a recognition or evaluation of a person's current level of happiness or accomplishment. Life satisfaction seems to come from within an individual based on personal values and what he or she believes is important. Multiple studies in various cultures have shown that an emphasis on materialism—money, possessions, affluence, class, "things," technology, even who you pride yourself on hanging out with—does not appear to be linked with higher levels of life satisfaction.

Fact. Both hope and optimism are linked to higher levels of life satisfaction. Also, a mindset that looks favorably on one's life and overall accomplishments rather than depending on one's current, fleeting, or momentary feelings. A balanced sense of self-esteem also plays a definite role in influencing life satisfaction—understanding that you have value simply because you exist. Identifying ways in which you have contributed positively to the lives of others reinforces an affirming mindset and self-talk style related to life satisfaction.

Fact. An "attitude of gratitude" has been linked with life satisfaction. Thankfulness has been shown to help an individual learn to delay gratification, a critical requisite for almost any type of success. Those who wrote "gratitude letters" to others who had made a difference in their lives were found to score higher on scales of happiness and lower on scales of depression. And the effects lasted for weeks! Melody Beattie's opinion is that gratitude unlocks the fullness of life. Oprah Winfrey has it right: *Concentrate on what you don't have and you'll never have enough.* (A scarcity mindset.) *Be thankful for what you have, and you'll tend to end up having more.* (A mindset and self-talk style of abundance.) Since everything begins in your brain, give thanks that you have one and a body to carry it around.

Fact. Joy cannot coexist simultaneously in the brain alongside anger, fear, or sadness. A mindset of joyful thankfulness promotes congruence of thoughts, emotions, and feelings, which tends to increase life satisfaction, reinforce gratefulness, improve problem solving, provide an antidote for fear, and enhance both health and potential lifespan. Satisfaction seems to increase as people age, especially as they become wiser and more knowledgeable, and practically apply what they have learned. Interestingly, studies have shown that morning-oriented individuals (sometimes referred to as "larks") tend to show higher levels of life satisfaction than do evening-oriented individuals (often called "night owls").

Fact. Those with high levels of life satisfaction typically exhibit a positive mindset and a good superego: they take excellent care of themselves *and* also are concerned with the well-being of others. They take appropriate steps to keep their own "cup" full, which allows them to share from an overflowing supply rather than from a deep well of unmet needs. Find ways to "give back" to Planet Earth, its inhabitants (people as well as creatures), and the environments needed to sustain life. Think ahead. Do whatever you can to help ensure a quality life for the next generation, and the next, and the next …

Fact. Craft your own personal vision. That's part of life satisfaction. Hone your spirituality—the spirit with which you live life. Do something every day to evoke a sense of awe in your brain and heart; then pass it on. It only takes a moment to smile, to lift someone's spirit, to make a positive difference in another person's life and, in the process, make a positive difference in your own life. Volunteer. Perform random acts of kindness. Be creative. Make a difference. (The sky is the limit!) Spread your metaphorical wings, give thanks—and fly!

Fact. Life satisfaction *matters!*

**Life satisfaction is a critical key,
To promote wellness and longevity.
Gratitude can be the spring,
To keep the day invigorating.**

LLM—Just the Facts!

"Life is a real kick in the bootie—and then *you* kick off," barked the tiny fox, irritably.

"What ruffled your fur this time" asked his uncle, accustomed to such outbursts from this tiny member of the skulk.

"Lots!" barked the tiny fox. "Got a burr stuck between my toes. My pathetic sister snored all night. My selfish brother grabbed the lion's share of breakfast. I pulled the short straw for chores today, plus I just stepped on a rock and hurt my paw. I say, life is rough and then you die!"

"Focusing on irritants can turn them into proverbial mountains in a nanosecond," said the uncle patiently. "Change your thoughts, change your life. There's always something for which to be grateful. Find it and give thanks."

"In my case that would be zip, nada, zero!" barked the tiny fox, rudely—that is, until they rounded a corner and unexpectedly came upon the remains of a cousin (several times removed), smashed in a cruel trap.

"Nothing to be done about this now," said the uncle. "Most, unfortunate, I say … *most* unfortunate indeed …"

"Ah-h-h. Methinks I will *rethink* that thankfulness stuff," murmured the tiny fox.

15—After the Facts …

 It has been said that many people perish for lack of knowledge—not from lack of information. After all, this *is* the "Information Age."

Information is simply information unless and until an individual chooses to turn it into knowledge and personally apply it on a daily basis. All things being equal, your basic lifestyle is a choice—*yours*!—especially in adulthood. You are the only one who can choose a healthy longevity lifestyle for *you*.

Be aware of genetics but recognize that's only worth 30 percent. Concentrate on epigenetics, the 70 percent! A longevity lifestyle can help you *prevent* what is preventable, *reduce the risk* for what isn't totally preventable, and *deal more effectively* with what was not or could not be prevented.

Many have taken less than optimum care of the brain and body leased to them for use on this planet. They are both important! Thomas Alva Edison believed that your brain is so valuable that your body's "chief function" is to transport your brain safely from place to place. They both need to be cared for carefully.

It isn't uncommon to hear individuals say, "If I had known what my lifestyle choices would cost me in health, productivity, relationships, and length, I'm quite sure I would have made some different choices." If that describes you, first, forgive yourself.

As Herbert Benson, MD, internationally known cardiologist, researcher, and author, describes it, "*An inability to forgive yourself and others for errors and mistakes is harmful to your health, relationships, and maybe even to longevity.*"

Desmond Tutu believed that without forgiveness there is no future. According to Gandhi, the weak can never forgive. Forgiveness is an attribute of the *strong*. You can be *both* strong *and* forgiving! Unforgiveness is costly—especially for the brain— in terms of health and longevity.

Mark Twain had it right. The secret of getting ahead is getting started. And the secret of getting started is breaking complex and seemingly overwhelming tasks into small manageable ones. Then, start on the first one. You know the fourteen components. Pick one not already part of your lifestyle. Think of it as a manageable task and get started. Implement it, consistently. When that one is firmly in place— typically after about twelve weeks—select another component and replicate the process.

Understand that what you do *today* will influence not only your tomorrows but also your overall future— and sometimes whether you'll even have a happy, healthy, and successful future. Recognize the importance of reinforcing your strategies through regular review and repetition. That is part of the exponential success formula.

Be very clear, there has never been a brain exactly like yours, nor will there ever be again. Matter of fact, same goes for your body. Together, your brain and body, are one-of-a-kind. That's exciting!

So, where to from here with your unique brain and body?

To a thriving future, of course—created by you!

Start now and turn information into knowledge, then practically apply it every day for the rest of your life. Applied knowledge drives behaviors, which impact your actions, which influence your health, wellness, and longevity. Make your life count. Leave a positive and memorable legacy. If you can "see it," likely you can "achieve it."

A longevity lifestyle . . . *matters!*

Now you have strategies one thru fourteen,
Each plays a part in a life serene.
You're the only person who can do it for you,
Picture your future—then make it come true.

LLM—Just the Facts!

"Ahoy, Caterpillar, I see you've begun your metamorphosis," said Praying Mantis.

"Duh," replied Caterpillar. "What was your first clue? My hanging upside down? Or my spinning silk to make a cocoon?"

"Always wondered what happens inside that shiny chrysalis," said Praying Mantis.

"If you must know," said Caterpillar, "I release enzymes that dissolve me into a caterpillar stew—except for a few pre-programed discs."

"And what do these pre-programmed discs do, pray tell?" asked Praying Mantis.

"They provide instructions to reconstruct the stew into all the parts I need as a Monarch Butterfly."

"Yuk," said Praying Mantis. "I would never go through such a disgusting process."

"Oh it's worth it," said Caterpillar. "When I emerge, I will be able to visit places I've only dreamed about instead of being earth-bound."

"Maybe I'll eat you," said Praying Mantis.

"Doubtful," said Caterpillar. "Doubtful. I'm able to remember lessons I learned before I spun my cocoon. One was this: Avoid a praying mantis. It'll be even easier to do that with my new wings!"

Author Facts & Resources

 **Arlene R. Taylor, PhD**, is sometimes referred to as the *brain guru.* A brain-function specialist, author, and international speaker, she specializes in presenting the complex topic of brain function in ways that help individuals more easily grasp and implement practical strategies to help them thrive. A sought-after presenter, Taylor is a member of the National Speakers Association, and lists with the Professional Speakers Bureau International.

Taylor is founder and president of Realizations, Inc., a 501 (c) (3) non-profit corporation that engages in brain function research and provides related educational resources. She has a Bachelor's in Nursing, a Master's in Epidemiology and Health Education, and two earned doctorates.

Dr. Taylor believes that nothing is more important than investing in your brain-body. Creating and maintaining a brain-based *Longevity Lifestyle* not only begins in the brain but is the key to success— helping you stay healthier and younger for longer. While encouraging individuals to be aware of their genetics, Taylor focuses on epigenetics that impacts wellness and potential lifespan to the tune of about seventy percent—and on the role of perceptions.

Contact Taylor at www.ArleneTaylor.org

 **Steve Horton, M.Div., MPH,** is enthusiastic about health and wellness, believing that a *Longevity Lifestyle* is not only possible, but can also be effective and enjoyable. Even fun! His goal is to provide educational resources in a stimulating, easy-to understand, and practical-to-apply format. As part of a lifelong commitment, the information and strategies can help people in the community become more aware of simple lifestyle changes to benefit their overall health, increase the likelihood of avoiding preventable diseases, and reduce symptoms of existing chronic illnesses.

Horton has two earned Master's. He is CEO of Pacific Health Education Center, a 501 (c) (3) non-profit corporation that exists to promote health and disease prevention both locally and abroad through education and service to others.

Contact Horton at www.PacificHealth.org

**With appropriate motivation,
education, practical application, and
the right use of their brains,
individuals may feel better, look better,
think more clearly, and
live healthier lives for longer.**

Resources

- *Longevity Lifestyle Matters (LLM)—2nd Edition (in process)*
- *Longevity Lifestyle Matters*—paperback, eBook, audiobook)
- *LLM—Companion Notebook* (paperback, eBook)
- *LLM 12-week Program*

- *Adventures of the Longevity Mystery Club* (paperback, eBook, audiobook)
- *Adventures of Aimi* (paperback, eBook, audiobook)
- *Adventures of Stella* (paperback, eBook, audiobook)

- *Chronicles of the Alabaster Owl* (paperback, eBook; audiobook in process)
- *Chronicles of the Jungle King* (paperback, eBook; audiobook in process)
- *Chronicles of the Littlest Dolphin* (paperback, eBook; audiobook in process)

- *Your Brain Has a Bent (Not a Dent)* 3rd Edition (paperback, eBook, Kindle, audiobook)

- *Brain Benders*: brain aerobic exercises (paperback)

- *Brain Music* (in process)

- *I Chose Hope—and that made the difference* (in process)

- *Age-Proofing Your Brain—21 Factors You Can Control,* 2nd Edition (paperback, eBook, Kindle, audiobook)

- *Beyond the House of Silence* (paperback, eBook; audiobook in process)

- *Age-Proofing Your Memory: Ultimate* (paperback, eBook)
- *Age-Proofing Your Memory: Scripture* (paperback, eBook)
- *Age-Proofing Your Memory: Mormon* (paperback)
- *Age-Proofing Your Memory: Catholic* (paperback)

Paperbacks, eBooks, audiobooks, and DVDs are distributed by Pacific Health Education Center:
www.PacificHealth.org/store/
661.633.5300

Paperbacks, Kindles, eBooks, and some DVDs are available at:
www.amazon.com

—The End—

Or perhaps

—The Beginning—

Made in the USA
San Bernardino, CA
07 April 2019